Y0-EEC-089

PITT POETRY SERIES

Ed Ochester, Editor

The Double Truth

Chard deNiord

University of Pittsburgh Press

Published by the University of Pittsburgh Press, Pittsburgh, PA 15260

Copyright © 2011, Chard deNiord

Manufactured in the United States of America

Printed on acid-free paper

10 9 8 7 6 5 4 3 2 1

ISBN 13: 978-0-8229-6134-5

ISBN 10: 0-8229-6134-2

for Liz

and in memory of my father

Richard N. deNiord Jr.

Why did you lie to me?
I always thought I told the truth.
Why did you lie to me?
Because the truth lies like nothing else and I love the truth.

—from "Elegy for My Father," Mark Strand

I got a bird that whistles
I got a bird that sings.

—from "Corrina, Corrina," Bob Dylan

CONTENTS

I

What a Doll Am I

I rise naked each morning and stand
at the window with arms outstretched
and feet apart like da Vinci's figure in the circle
and wait for the day's attendants to dress me
in garments they choose for that morning—
a shroud one day, a coat of lead the next.
What a doll am I to these attendants
whose only task is to remind me
day after day of who I am:
that man or woman I think I'm not.

Trailer

The guests are floating in the lobby,
walking but also gliding to the front desk
then away, checking in, checking out,
muscular souls adorned in cotton,
wool, and rayon, chewing the future
inside their heads, slicing the air
with ironed pleats, avoiding the camera
at every turn so as, so as to get it right
this time, which is the first time.
"First cut, best cut!" the director shouts
since this is also a silent film for the deaf
and therefore everyone. His aim
is to get the cast to see what they've
been missing, to disregard the very sounds
that they don't hear to begin with,
but would notice immediately
if they were gone. See how they glide
on the ether above the floor.
The insouciance, Lord. The insouciance!
They are all here in the magic of the set,
every soul in the guise of a guest
going about her business, a rendezvous here,
an assignation there, the solitary sipping
at the bar. Someone striking appears
at the door. The rain outside beats down
on the streets with terrible force until all
you can hear is the roar of the sky as it passes
above, and then below, on its narrow tracks.

Renunciation

A small dark cloud in the shape of *no*
appeared at the edge of the otherwise clear October
sky, then floated as an answer inside my head
to a question that I forgot, as if my mind
and sky were one, but without a breeze to blow
the *no* into something else, anything else
beyond the *little cause* inscribed across
the earth. *What a sky is the mind,* I thought. *What a field
the heart.* And the more I thought, the larger the cloud
became, as if I knew from the start I couldn't
love for long, much less forever as the blue
appeared to want. As if the sky were ready
to remove its veil at the sign of the smallest cloud,
defer to the sudden drop of darkness again.

Club Erebus

> Death is the mother of beauty.
> —WALLACE STEVENS

They emerged from a door that wasn't a door
and floated across the room to the stage
which they ascended and began to sway
and bend and turn with only their G-strings on.
I sat at the bar drinking gin and smoking
a cigar, watching them work beneath
the lights, accept the funds of happy men
who took great care in folding their bills
like miniature towels inside the belts
around their thighs that went *k'ching,*
k'ching, until rings of bills adorned
their thighs and the music stopped
for a moment, long enough for them
to disappear into the dark of the high
stone door at the end of the stage
where they waved good-bye, good-bye
and then were gone beneath the world
like the ghosts they were, to rest for a while,
the longest time, before returning live
to die again as they had before.

They Are Most at Home

They are most at home in the sea,
the way their bodies embody water,
whether or not they can swim
with ease, which they can't,
but like water, their bodies flow
and purl and bend in such a way
you want to swim in them and fish
for marlin and cast your nets and dive
for oysters and study their currents
and surf their waves and taste their salt.
Each garment they wear is a bathing suit.
They are the genius of water that stains
the water with the blood of men
who sought the land and forced
them to follow. They are the body
of water from which a body comes.

Pitch

There are four men with guns in a boat just offshore at night.
They're on a mission to survey the beach for an imminent invasion.
They are the good guys and the odds are against them.
They're in the moment of the other life, the eternal present
in which they know they aren't going to live.
The elements conspire to bring out the beauty of the Pacific night,
St. Elmo's fire in a distant rigging, phosphorescence on the waves.
It's a moment when we're willing to believe almost anything.
One of the soldiers leans over the bow and retrieves a bottle
with a message inside from his love. He reads it silently
and begins to weep. We've known from the start that he's the one
who's going to die, who must be sacrificed in the end for our beliefs.
We can't know at this moment whether he'll be shot or stabbed,
whether he'll suffer for long or die quickly on the beach.
He has a sweet face, large shoulders, and a hitch in his speech.
He pulls himself together and wipes his cheeks with the back of his hand,
folds the message along its crease, then slips it in his pocket.
The water laps against the boat. The oars dip in and out.
Music plays inside a cloud. We know the ending before it starts
but need to see these men in the open boat as if we were ignorant
of the outcome. We need to see what happened again in order to separate
the facts from life. We have no idea what any of the men were really like
as they paddled to shore that night. What any of them said or did before
they landed and measured the beach, then paddled back without the kid.

The Police

We were in bed when a knock came at the door. Our bed was next to the front door since we had given up our only bedroom to our two children and partitioned off a part of our large living room with standing bookcases into a second bedroom for us. It was ten-thirty on a Sunday night. The knocks resounded hard and quick. I was reading Czeslaw Milosz's *The Witness of Poetry* in preparation for a seminar the next morning. My wife, Rachel, was reading Soren Kierkegaard's *The Concept of Irony*. "Who could that be?" I asked, rising naked from bed and putting on my kimono. I opened the door to find two police officers. "Come in gentlemen," I said. The uniformed men entered and stood over our bed. Rachel pulled the sheet up to her neck. I stood at the end of the bed. "We're here because a Mrs. Little called. She said she's been trying to reach you since yesterday, but the phone's been busy." I picked up the phone by the bed and heard a faint static through the receiver. "The phone *is* broken," I said. "We got in this evening, officer, from a weekend trip, and haven't used the phone since we got back. Maybe it was that tornado that knocked it out." The policemen stood sheepishly together. Rachel smiled with embarrassment for her mother. I, on the other hand, had a strange impulse to invite the two policemen to bed with us, but said instead, "Would it be too much to ask one of you to call Mrs. Little back to assure her that we are OK?" They were kind, Midwestern policemen who said they would be happy to do this. I imagined them climbing into bed with us and falling asleep, while we stripped them of their uniforms and put them on ourselves and held their empty weapons to our necks and heads and groins and kissed each other over their veteran bodies while they slept deeply in their exhaustion. We thanked these men for their prompt response to my mother-in-law's concern for us. I wanted also to tell them, *You have given me a larger sense of myself as well as assuring me of something I wondered about before, namely the inherent goodness of the police whose abruptness and armed appearance and lack of tact and laconic style I forgive this time because my mother-in-law was concerned about us and had nowhere else to turn except to you.* But I knew also that they didn't expect this and probably wouldn't have understood my sentiment exactly. Strangely, what I think they would have understood and probably responded to if their duty had not prevented them from getting too close to their public was an invitation to come to bed with us fully clothed, for it was late, they were tired, and this is what we wanted.

First Sex

As a child I hung from my belly
on a bar in the attic to feel
the pressure of the cool, round
iron against my groin.
Bar was the term I knew
for sex, although I knew
another word lay hidden
behind the letters *b*,
a, and *r*, but needed
to hang for a few more years
in the cedar closet between
the garments that were out of season
before I found the letters
s, *e*, and *x*
in the rebus of *bar*. Before
I dropped to the floor with so
much knowledge between my teeth
I could only whisper it
to the garments. Could only wonder
at the charge of my own current.
It came to me as I hung
like a worm in the chrysalis
of my desire: a voice inside
the pipe proclaiming the name
for what I felt, a sound
that caught the fish-like force
inside my gut and flew
with it across the sky.

April 1

There is a new quality in the air,
a sweet redolence from the first flowers
and pungent odor of soil emerging
from the thaw, that smell that spring passes
under your nose to wake you again,
more than wake you, stir you in such a way
that you recall the irony that kills,
the shadow in the drupe, the upswing
on the ward. How strange you think
at the time to think of your body as form,
a cloud, while also knowing that it will clear
into the blue. You laugh and a flower blooms
beside a door that opens onto a darkness
that is so vast no light can light it,
that is the zero against which everything
in this world is multiplied.

> History, you know, is one thing and our lives are something
> else.
> —OCTAVIO PAZ

In the old days when there was still a symbiosis in that magical city of Jews, Germans, and Czechs, all living together in peace and contrast around the same statues and fountains, I remember desiring only one thing, quality of life. I was a streetwise kid, unlike my brother, who went away to America for university and never returned. I was an anarchist and Jew who survived the war. I was John Wayne and Ronald Reagan in the summer of 1945 when I returned to Prague from London after flying twenty-four bombing missions in the Czech Air Force. I wore a Smith and Wesson at my side and went everywhere in my uniform because no one was making clothes yet; the factories had all shut down.

I was sitting at a café one late afternoon with three friends when I looked over at a table across from us and saw three beautiful girls. I told my friends, "The one with the smoky eyes is mine." We introduced ourselves, then sat together for a while in the warm afternoon sun. My friend Jaraslav said, "It's such a beautiful evening. Why don't we all go for a walk?"

The girl with the smoky eyes and I walked down to the river where I took off all my clothes and went swimming. I can still feel that water and see the sun setting over the city. It was a moment I had been waiting for without knowing what it was going to be like. I had swum naked in the river before, grown up in Prague, and watched plenty of sunsets, but suddenly I felt I was seeing the city for the first time. A powerful nostalgia overwhelmed me. I saw the old city superimposed on the new one, that I was a lucky witness of the irrevocable loss. How was I now to recall that great city whose buildings still cast the same shadows through which Kafka, Brod, Rilke, Mahler, Kisch, Mucha, Čapel, Dvorak, Hašek, Škvorecký, Werfel, and Hrabal had walked, thought, and composed, if for just for a moment, in that cultural flowering we are unlikely ever to see

again? My memory proved itself better than I thought as I recalled the looks of faces and heights of the fountains. I wept as I swam. I committed myself in that moment to preserve the memory of the old city, to hold a mirror up to the war and cut off its head, to teach architecture and history together as the same course, discuss what happened in these buildings, who was arrested where and in what room, who wrote what in which study. My favorite view is that of Kafka's, the relief of the lamb above the large window across the street from his study, that lamb he wrote about in its awkward prone position with unvanquished dignity, innocence, and absurdity. I was at a great turning point in history, between one fascist regime and another, but all I could see was the city and the river and the girl with smoky eyes lying on the bank under the trees.

When I was through swimming, I sat next to the girl in the twilight and stared at the river, fixing one eye on the current and the other on the liquid reflections of trees and buildings. We didn't talk for some time, and then she turned to me and said, "Pin me like a butterfly." So I did.

Afterwards, we went to her house to meet her parents. They prepared a gorgeous meal for us. A large plant with thick leaves and full blossoms occupied the center of the table, preventing me from seeing my love on the other side. I did something foolish then. I took out my knife and cut the plant in two with one stroke. This was my mentality from the war. Her mother leaned back in her chair with an expression of shock and said, "How awful." Her father said nothing but put his hand gently on mine and nodded with compassion, as if to restrain me further. I stood up and excused myself, thanking them for their hospitality. I showed myself to the door, and then, when I was outside, I ran from that house and never returned.

Instructions for Telling the Truth

Begin by removing one article of clothing at a time, slowly,
until nothing's left to take off and no one's watching.
Patience, patience, as your words replace your garments
and suddenly you're standing alone in the square
like a flower that speaks in silence with so many tongues.

The Fire in the Distance

Just when the match between the top contenders
heats up in the third set, a cloud of smoke rises
from behind a berm in the distance, distracting
the announcers in their booth above the stadium,
for they are more curious about the fire
than the highly anticipated match between the number
one and two players in the world. The fire has flared up
out of nowhere and threatens to burn down what appears
to be a barn, although it's hard to tell from here,
while the two contenders hit the ball back and forth
with a brilliance that we, the viewers, have grown
accustomed to. We also grow more interested in the fire
as the announcers wonder during a crossover
if it's a house instead of a barn that's ablaze.
We're suddenly reminded by other marginal events
of the *thin partitions* that surround our field of vision,
whether imagined or real, as well as of the fertile strangeness
that draws our attention every time within the realm
of the ordinary—a fire here, a coup d'état there—
always something encroaching from the outside,
which is also the main event somewhere else,
but contiguous to the stadium, inching or zooming
toward center court. In the meantime, everyone looks
like a parody of someone else in this gestalt—boyfriend,
girlfriend, former mayor. One of the players eventually wins,
although it's hard to remember which one, while the fire grows
in strength in everyone's mind like memory itself with its odd,
acquisitive consumption of things on the edge that occur
mysteriously but nonetheless contain a psychic fuel
that feeds a *hard gemlike flame*. Since the announcers know
nothing substantive about the fire, except that it exists
with the same miraculous presence as the first fire

Prometheus brought down at the risk of his life,
their producers advise them to turn their attention
back to the match. The idiosyncratic rules and regulations
of the tournament stand in contrast to the fire
that shows no regard for the artificial order.
The audience watches this specific future unfold
in the form of a game, where contingencies occur also,
yes, but only as a residue of the players' skill:
a net cord here, a lucky wood there, and yet,
no matter how much I, a judge in my own chair,
admonish the announcers for mentioning the fire,
I appreciate their curiosity for something out of the ordinary,
for I too would want to know more about the smoke
on the horizon, and say so on the air. "There's a fire
in the distance," I'd say, "although none of us
can see from here just what it is that's burning."

The Silence

Soon enough you will come to see the vanity
of feeling compelled to explain yourself
or take something back you can't take back.
You will learn to throw your voice into the silence.
To let it speak for you in the trees and rivers.
You will come to recognize it as darkness's sister,
how together they form the evening and sweep
the earth like the hem of a widow's dress.
You will come to find yourself in a folding chair
at the edge of the world staring at candles
on the long horizon, glimmering, glimmering.
With a gimlet in one hand and a rifle in the other,
you will watch yourself disappear in the gaze
of a squirrel who is really an angel assigned
by his Lord to test your soul in the gloaming
with the swish of his tail and chatter, chatter.
Shoot me again. Shoot me again.
And you will have to see if you can keep
the barrel down as the darkness falls
at the side of silence, singing, singing.

II

Ockham Applies His Razor to the Thought of Aquinas

I ❧
Proof from Motion

If you begin with the wind,
you wonder of course
where it begins,
what difficult force
behind the scenes
denies itself to the point
of being beyond a thing,
which is to say
the mind defeats itself
with thoughts that turn
against each other, over and over,
until they reach a point
where they expire,
which is the point for those obsessed
with proving things,
who say they see in certain terms
but cannot see for seeing.
Take a domino for instance
that does not move
unless it's moved by something else;
it's fixed in its potential
and cannot be both moved and moving.
If everything has absence then in its potential,
the question is, what moved initially?
What contradiction moves a thing
but does not need another thing
to set it off?
God, he says.
Witness then how reason leads

to nothing, as if the sky
were an infinite curtain
both open and closed.
As if this stream of traffic
were both still and moving.

II ☙

Proof from Efficient Cause

If nothing can precede itself
then it depends on something else
to bring it into being.
Since we are too conditioned to
the tooth and foul,
we cannot view an infinite past
without a cause.
We cannot think of shadows as real
reflecting objects in an actual world.
We live by experience or not at all.
Something moved of its own accord
with a cause at first, something
for whom size was insignificant,
a point perhaps without a place
except its own.
But if you reduce a cause to origin
you must use time to stump infinity;
infinity is the problem, see,
the high conundrum in which
He does not function
as a primal anything,
and yet He cannot be in time
and also free of time
as perfectly unchangeable,
which is why He is eternal,

that is, infinite with an attitude,
not unlike the man
who just passed me in his topcoat
and suit, so insouciant and armed,
no doubt, but human for now.
This logical conclusion of endless regression
is absurd therefore
without a God whose nature confounds,
who is no less or more
than the sum of logic
that leaves a pilgrim cold.

III ॐ
Proof from Necessary versus Possible Being

God is not possessive,
like a creature that *has* its being.
Rather He *is* His being,
perfectly alone, autonomous and pure.
He is His own necessity
which everything in turn
inherits as form.
What we observe is that reflection
of both His cause and need:
what we know but cannot explain
for passing through a fire
that turns the body itself
into a flame that burns
the merely possible
like so much chaff.
He could have saved himself
with this confession:
My logic was a scaffold
in lieu of faith,

my cake for eating too.
His language is the thing
that's missing like a soul:
no quick of reification,
no entry that says:
the woods rehearse
from tree to tree
as if to say
creation is the step where
a thing would be if it could be
both here and there like her
the one who will not dance with me
I view the park where all that moves
with the grace of trees is dreamed
at first conceived delivered whole
by a single word

IV ☙

Proof from the Degrees of Perfection

If all my intelligence
finally leads to ignorance,
profound as it may be,
the ultimate degree, for instance,
the end of all exponents,
then what is left to lift my spirits?
A fire in space?
A self-moving hand?
See how convinced it is
of its own designs
arriving at ends defying its means.
Such thinking fails at paradox
for not imagining first
the existence of something real

that isn't there: a sea in the sky,
the turtle beneath,
for not considering the heart
that wants to believe,
for changing the language
from lilies to cause, wine to proof,
bread to degrees,
for never swimming in the river
that doesn't end, or kissing another
in the darkness of your room
where all you can see
is the trick of flesh
and all you can say
is *I crave this death.*
Nothing is so clean or pure or first
that has the idea of earth.
What God would submit to reasonable proof?
I hear a silent voice proclaim,
Aquinas has tried to define us,
my hosts and me, put on a weight
exceeding stars, too heavy
for even me to lift
from his unvarnished chair.

  V ☙

  Proof from the Order of the Universe

Read a psalm, study a spider,
conclude from everything
that works without a thought
another thought without a mind
that is a force of reason,
that is visible up to a point
before it blurs then disappears.

This blur is God, this sense
on the other side achieved
by reasons that destroy themselves.
This bright deduction that only confirms
the logical end of a working mind.
This madness blind to the turns
of negative routes where the curtain falls
each time to save us from the face
that scrambles eyes and stops the heart.

What Beauty Knows about Itself

That it is a genius in its diversity and therefore ruthless.
That it is not enough in the end to hold the beloved,
although it seems to be at first, more than seems.
That it hosts a worm that is capable of consuming the heart in a day.
That it is perishable, like fruit, if left out too long.
That it needs a sister, like Antigone, to add something essential
to its otherwise pusillanimous character.
That it is transcendent form, criminal catalyst.
That it might as well be motherless since death is its mother.
That it fades much quicker than it appears.

From the Curriculum of a Serpent

Search your heart for any trespass
you might have committed against
your neighbor, weighing each slight
and peccadillo on the scale of earth
beneath you, then remove the ballasts
of generous deeds from the mass of your
transgressions since they are timid birds
in the mind of your neighbor, flying off
on the wings of forgetfulness to leave
the dead weight of insult behind,
tipping the scale beyond its highest
number. Try next to guess
the number on which the sharp red
needle would settle if the numbers went
that high. Gaze down then if you can
to see how stuck is the needle
on the highest number, which is only
the partial weight of what you feared
was true about the heft of even
the smallest hurt on the scale of earth
that stretches out before you.

Puritan in Flight

He gazed at the Arctic below
from his window seat, which made
him think of the cotton throws
that sinners used to cover
the arms of pulpits and chairs.
How weary he'd grown in his
own time, so half at home
in the hum of planes. *Better*
to suffer the pain of skin
on oak than blindfold an elbow
with antimacassars. It kept him
aloft, this perfect thought,
as he gazed at the arm of the Arctic
chair and leaned on it
in the atmosphere, brushed off
the snow with a whisk of mind
until the ice appeared
and he slept for a while inside
the sky with great unknowing.

At the Socratic Sugarhouse

I said "The steam is like a ghost
in the sugarhouse," and you said
that didn't mean anything to you
since you didn't believe in ghosts.
So I said, "How about a cloud then,"
and you said, "But it isn't a cloud
either. It's steam. Why do you want
to make it something it isn't?"
"I was only imagining," I said.
"Don't you ever imagine?"
"What for?"
                    "To see things."
"I see plenty. It's dangerous
to see more than what's there."
"But if you don't, you don't see
what's there."
                    "Like ghosts?"
"Well, yes, ghosts and other things.
If I said to you that the steam
is a ghost that haunts this house,
what would you say?"
                    "I'd say
you're crazy. What's real is here
and every place else."
                    "I'm not
saying it isn't. I think the same,
but what about those things
you can't see?"
                    "You've lost me
now. You'd better keep your mind
on the pan. Too much thinking

ruins the syrup."
                    "I'm looking back
and ahead at the same time when I stare
at the sap. My mind's the fire
that boils the sap that turns
to syrup."
                    "That sounds nice enough
but crazier still than what you said
before about the ghosts and clouds.
Now run that off before it burns."
"Do you think that someone
who thought that steam was like
nothing else in the world invented
syrup? That's what I mean by looking
back, wondering what someone saw
in something that wasn't yet real
but hidden there. So when I look
at the steam and see a ghost,
I'm only dreaming of course.
I know it's steam, but I'm also
saying there are things inside
of things."
                    "The world's the way
it is—always knowable in the end.
Always hard with evidence
if you look close enough.
I looked at something once
and called it *sugar* by mistake.
The little sweetness we get
comes from so much work:
forty gallons of sap to one of syrup.
You look at the steam and see
a ghost. I look at the steam
and see my grief. We're close

enough in that I guess,
so let's leave it there.
Either way, it comes to nothing
in the air above the roof."

The Bride as Scout

I ❧

I kept waking to the voices of reruns, cowboys mostly,
then drifting off to sleep.
                              I must have heard them also
in my sleep, for I dreamt of lawmen on the trail at night
lying around a fire discussing a plan for tracking
their man through the canyon tomorrow.
                              It was
their wisdom to sleep that gave me hope in my sleep
for capturing the man, for bringing justice to the land
that was mostly wild.
                              The low, desultory tones
of their voices sang to me from the other side,
took the hand of my mind and led me over.
                              I was
asleep but awake to myself in an empty bed that was also
the shore of a swollen river.

II ❧

                              I spied the man on the shore
and went to him with a blanket and pillow.
                              Lay down
beside him on the lam and whispered, "They're not far behind,
my love, but we can lose them."
                              He was my fugitive
in the hills, wanted, wanted.
                              I had the power as my reward

to read the stars as good-bye letters.
                                    "Come back. Come
back," I cried to the hole in the morning.
                                        "In the time
it takes to make an arrest, I will have slept with him forever."

A History of Love's Body

Each morning I bared my ass
to the angel of numbness.
All beauty and business was she
in administering the cold cc's
with a smile that hurt. With hair
pulled back by a single pin
and wings tucked in to her body-
suit, she tapped the syringe
and made it squirt, sang
in French, froze my heart.
I kissed her on the mouth
and said, "Au revoir, my dear."
Pulled up my pants and buttoned
my shirt with the knowledge
of suffering, suffering, but that
was it; no feeling it inside my head
where I digressed on this and that
with turns of thought that left me stunned,
disinterested and smart, ready to write,
which I did, I did like a perfect bastard.
For a hundred years I took her shots
and won awards and always thought,
I feel enough, I feel enough,
when then it was a voice cried out
between my coughs,
both beautiful and true
as my dose wore off.

Both beautiful and untrue
without the benefit of morning.

Gird your loins, it warned,
for the onslaught of others as you, you.

35

And I was afraid.

Choose one at the start
and work from there.

And I was confused.

See how it remains itself
while also crossing over
to any number.

And I was emboldened.

I call it the math of the unfrozen heart.
I call it the consanguinity of minds released from fear.

And I was prepared.

But you must name it yourself
for it to mean anything at all.
Find your own words for the pain
that makes you whole—both you and another,
no matter how awkward or brief.

And I uttered a sound that made
no sense, but was indelible in the air,
a syllable was all that grew
in my throat, a diphthong for the pitch
of two songs at once, both joy and grief.

The Woe That Is in Friendship

In the sudden silence of his phone
he knew that something was wrong,
but not in general—with him, *him*.
He was born with the knowledge of his own problems,
but not the tools to solve them completely.
They wanted to tell him, then didn't, wisely—
his friends of so many years—not that he blamed them.
How awkward they must have felt in the smoke
of the steak and chicken their last time over.
How free they were that autumn to sit alone
on their separate porches and stare at the trees.
Watch the leaves fall to the ground like unmailed letters.
Sail like clouds into the clean, ecstatic future.

Dear George

Why should I kiss you, honey bear,
after you've proclaimed both near and far,
"When I talk about peace, I'm really talkin' about war"?

And why should I sit on your lap, booboo,
when you have no idea who Gilgamesh was
or his beloved Enkidu?

And *how should I presume*, cupcake,
when you can't recall having made a single mistake?

And why should I return with you, pomegranate,
when your heart's as hard as Rutland granite?

And why should I draw on your back, sweetheart,
when you can't even *lie down where the ladders start*?

And why should I tell you what the serpent said, sugar beet,
when the frogs are dying, but you don't feel the heat?

And why would I want to unravel my knitting, peanut,
when you cry "freedom" from every window, but you don't mean it?

And why should I come home, six pack,
when I'm with Erishkigal in the black zone of Iraq?

The Soul Addresses Her Beloved in the Non-Green Zone

> Nor did it do me any good to summon
> Inspirations for him, with which I called him
> In dreams and otherwise, so little he heeded them.
> —DANTE, *Purgatorio*, Canto 30, lines 133–36
>   (translated by W. S. Merwin)

That little girl in the surf
is your double—my love,
my enemy—with the difference
of another. Sacred then,
because there she is
when you turn your head,
sovereign, mysterious, good.
Do you see? Not yours.
My grief for you is equal
to the awe I feel for the little girl.
But why?

It is I-as-you, *you*,
whom you have lost
and cannot find without closing
your eyes, shutting your ears.
I am here on the curb.
No, there in the market.
Not I-as-you, but ten thousand things
that make you large,
the girl in the doorway, the boy
at his mother's side.
How to explain?

When I see the hammock
where I once lay behind your eyes
now filled with swords and *holy lines*,

I know you're dying already
inside your loaded body.
I know you're hosting a party
to which I'm not invited.

I tell you these things as your beloved
in the guise of a stranger
who speaks with a voice that does not rise
any higher than what you hear
in the silence of a snowy field.
Do you hear?

You have replaced me with a poet
who believes that paradise is a heaven
full of virgins singing your name.
I call to you across the hills
to be with me again in an empty room,
blind, deaf, and whole.
Restored.

It is you I love and miss.
See how human you are in the eyes
of the little girl who regards you with a smile.
See how invisible you are as a man
amidst the crowd.
Are you more angry at me than your enemy?
My constant chatter in the midst of war?
Forgive me.

You are so distant I can hear
my echoes inside of your bones.
I can feel your thumb on the button
that He has not withheld from you
in all His wisdom.

The Only Road

I was coming off the mountain
into the valley to get some gas in Keene
when suddenly I saw that this was it.
That there was no paradise beyond this mountain
that doubles as sky and earth.
I put the truck in neutral and glided for a while
in the firmament.
I hardly had to steer or think.
I regarded the clouds as pages on which
I had yet to write so much and nothing.
The road descended like a long, black ribbon
into the valley of Connecticut.
I was going forth and coming back
on the same long highway on which I'm still
at the speed of light.
I was leaving a trail of invisible tracks
on the only road that leads to Keene
and then Vermont.

Yet so as by Fire

For H. B.

If any man's work shall be burned, he shall suffer loss:
but he himself shall be saved, yet so as by fire.
—1 CORINTHIANS 3:15

His fear was all and fuel.
So spread it did, the angel fire,
igniting the cedar that he himself
had laid beneath the diamonds,
gold, and straw. The beauty
of his raiment was a living
garb as he went up on his
ironic pyre, crackling.
Each organ screamed to enter
there in a saffron cloud,
then almost clear. All soul
was he in those alarms to keep
his bones aflame and heart attired.

Sunday Calls

The nurse calls to tell me on Sunday evenings
how he's doing.
                        How he's holding his own in front
of the window with a thousand channels behind
the one that saves his screen with snow, fish houses,
and eagles.
                        How the days hang above the ice as vast
recycled pages on which he writes in invisible ink.
How the sun arcs across the sky, then breaks like a plate
above the horizon.
                        How the temperature drops
below zero at dusk, then continues to fall till morning.
In this way she teaches me how to speak to him in his sleep
at his home in Minnesota, which is the same, she says,
as talking to a friend you've never met, but grown close to
nonetheless from hearing his voice.
                                        I hear the snow
falling as she holds the phone outside the window.
Silence is the sound of snow falling on snow, I think
as I listen to the flakes inside the air before she closes
the window.
                        "I'm thinking of walleye in their sleep,"
I tell my father.
                        "Of catching them as they dream,
then throwing them back in the hole I drilled by hand
with the auger you gave me as a child, whose handle is stained
with blood from my turning it so many times into the ice
of Bad Medicine."
                        I wait for her voice to return, then say,
"Just this for now since any more would disappear the lake
inside his head on which he builds a house for us to fish
throughout the winter."

III

Coyotes

Twenty or more in the meadow.
I ran down to meet them.
Buried my face in their sides.
Smelled their urine and sex.
Ran beside them.
Alas,
descended.
Conversed with souls,
both human and animal.
Read the book of sticks
from beginning to end.
Rose up again
in the form of coyote.
Killed a deer.
Pulled muscle from bone.
Slept in the snow.
Howled at the moon.

The Thinker

slithered so smoothly it seemed the ground was moving
beneath her as she wound across the earth to coil
on her throne, which was anywhere she stopped
to rest like a rope in sexual skin and heal
the ground, detect a wind before it arrived,
record degrees inside her blood. Circumference
upon circumference was she as she went out, no part
from which to draw a larger thing, but whole
as she was in a uniform of chevrons and stripes. Cold eye
with a body that wrapped the earth in sleeves
of former selves. Sensei par excellence
with a tongue that spoke the double truth
as an order no creature with legs or arms could follow.

The Golden Herd

The cows were bellowing again in the meadow,
so I went down to them through the maples
like the herder I wasn't to see what was wrong,
for something had to be wrong the way
they were lowing so loud in the distance
as if to sound the alarm of locusts or coyotes.
As if they were the golden herd of Apollo
and Odysseus's men had just arrived to slaughter them.
But there they were as usual in their huddle,
except for one who had wandered off
and was grazing by the beaver pond in a calm,
eternal manner. What could I know
of their bovine moods, that calculus that lay
embedded in the marrow of their skulls
like a problem beyond my solving, their sudden
explosive bellowing for what appeared to be no reason,
as if they needed no reason as a reason for bellowing
at nothing on this otherwise peaceful, April morning?

Virgil's Bees

Virgil made up almost all of what he wrote
about the bees: how the queen is a king in fact,
how moisture in the softened bones
of a slaughtered heifer spawns a new hive
in the season when the zephyrs first ruffle the waves.
If we're always wrong about something
in the age in which we live,
then how is something we believe today
about ourselves any less foolish
than what Virgil believed about the bees?
And why do we need to believe them still—
those Latin lines—when we know they are not true?

In a Dark Wood

I crossed the stream that had grown cloudy in the heat
of August.
                        I watched a trout and crawfish swim
in the shallow pool beneath the roots of a willow tree,
then followed a path into a forest of maple, oak, and birch.
When I stopped to listen, I heard a thrush in the understory
singing to his mate.
                        A breeze blew through the canopies
of the highest trees.
                        A red-tailed hawk circled the sky in wider
and wider circles.
                        Gazing down at the dark, damp earth,
I noticed where a moose had walked on the path before veering
off into the woods.
                        A spider had spun her web across the trail
between one ironwood and another.
                                        I ducked beneath
and continued to walk, less and less sure of how I had entered
these woods
                        All I could think as a man who'd lived before,
but not really, was how full of sleep I had been at that moment
when I left the house.
                        How far away for being so near
was the mountain that rose before me.
                                        I observed *the pass*
which never yet let anyone go alive
                                        and thought of the spider that had spun
her web across the path behind me.
                                        How to ride the air
with so much thought?
                        How to swim beyond the sharks
inside the lake of my own heart?

Storm Cloud

I observed the dark cloud expanding
above the ridge as I folded the laundry
and admitted to myself that I know
far less than the ant or spider.
For how long did I make this error
of thinking I knew more than the creatures?
Of not enjoying the smallest chores?
Now that I have imagined myself
from above, I see my tasks as blessings
in the ruse of motions, as if the world
were invisible to the dead and I were
merely dancing for them on an empty
stage from a great, great distance
that is also near, adjusting my glasses,
folding a towel, looking up.

The Percherons

My sister and I went out to them with sugar
cubes and bridled their heads when they bent down
to eat from our palms. We led them over
to the long white fence on which we climbed
to the topmost rail, then threw our legs
across their backs, clutching the reins to steady
ourselves against their girth, steering them out
into the hills until we were lost, or thought
we were, only to find ourselves at Judith
Creek or Holcomb Rock where we'd turn back
in the early dark, gripping their manes, crouching
low, galloping hard on the high soft
road across the fields to the open barn.

The Animals

I talked back to a cow in the upper field.
Patted her brow as she lowed in the barn.
I was mesmerized also by the chickens
in the yard as they strutted and pecked the ground.
I sat at the tables of all the animals to learn
their letters: the long *e* of the hawk,
the broad *a* of the crow, the diphthong
of the moose. I grasped the goodness
in their natures, whether wild or tame.
They were the blessed, dumb angels of earth.
Why was I so moved by the mere opening
of a beak, twitch of a flank, wiggle of a tail?
They brought me tokens of myself—a cold eye here,
a Christlikeness there. I was enlarged by a bee,
enlightened by a mouse. Nothing I did
returned to them what they brought to me.
They were the geniuses of paradise still.
I watched them *half the day long* as they swam
and leapt and crawled in their going forth.
I called each one by name, although
they did not come, except for the dog.
I pulled them from a thicket and prayed
as they lay on a stone and bled.

August 17

I heard the whistle of winter blow
as my chain saw howled in August
inside the maple I felled last fall
and let sit for a year in sections
before sawing it into logs for splitting.
My sweat mixed in with the maple,
so I was acrid, acrid. Never enough
wood for winter, although there is,
even when the frost extends to the end
of April and the pile diminishes
to half a cord. You can't fell a dozen trees
that have to season a couple of years
and feel you've felled enough.
Winter freezes more than your feet
and fingers, also your eyes in an inward stare.
You know in either the heat of August
or the warmth of the shut-down stove
in March that winter is always ahead,
no matter the season, bearing down
with a schedule that's written in white
and is more than punctual: relentless,
long, and residual, that shakes the house
as it passes by as an engine hauling
ten thousand cars of coal and snow.

IV

After Marlowe

Come, my love, and indict the ground.
Depose the ants beside my head.
Subpoena the darkness inside their holes.
Cite the clouds and arraign the sky.
Arrest yourself on the same old charge.
Sit with me in the witness chair and al-
locate to the judge what the serpent knows
already but likes to hear again.
How you thought so hard for us both
you made me think for myself.
How what I've thought ever since
is shameful, dear, *shameful*, yes.
How godly she was, that creature in the tree
who spoke in your voice—that leg with legs
and a crack in her tongue for telling the truth.

Bare and Live

When we waded chest-deep into the river,
we carried the current to our eyes
with a charge that raised the bodies inside
our bodies to sky. Turned our veins
to voltage. Minnows nibbled at our groins
while a murder of crows cawed from a pine
their common knowledge, rough alarm.
We were in two places at once like a wire,
stretched out between the cathodes of our
desire. So bare and live the ether
hummed like a swarm inside the air.

This Ecstasy

It's not paradise I'm looking for
but the naming I hardly gave a thought to.
Call it the gift I carried in my loneliness
among the animals before I started
listening to the news. Call it the hint
I had about the knowledge that would explode.
In the meantime, which is real time
plus the past, you're swishing your skirt
and speaking French, which is more
than I can take, which I marvel at
like a boy from the most distant seat
in the Kronos Dome, where I am one
of so many now I see the point
of falling off. There're not enough seats
for us all to attend the eschaton.
This ecstasy that plants beauty
on my tongue, so that if it were
a wing, I'd be flying with the quickness
of a hummingbird and grace of a heron,
is so much mercy in light of the darkness
that comes. Who would say consolation?
Who would say dross? Not that anyone
would blame them. All night I hear
so many echoes in the forest I'm tempted
to look back, to save myself in hindsight,
where all I see is the absence of me.
Where all I hear is your voice,
which couldn't be more strange.
How to go on walking hand in hand
without our bodies on the path
we made for our feet, talking, talking?

In the Brief Time We Have Left

Let the ant live that's crossing the table.
Give me a kiss.
Give me another kiss.

After the Storm

> I will go to the bank by the wood . . .
> —WALT WHITMAN

The sky was drawn with purple clouds.
I headed barefoot down to the field
in only a robe, untied. The mud
oozed up between my toes
until the path became a stream
and I walked on coins the dead had spent.
Fireflies sparked in the ferns this late
in August, and an owl called out
somewhere like a hole with a god inside.
I was disappeared by the low, cool sweep
of clouds and complex darkness.
By the breath of animals inside the darkness.
By the dwelling of darkness inside the darkness.
I followed the trail by feel to the edge
of the stream, where I could see across,
just barely, to the uncut grass of the meadow.
The bridge had held somehow in the surge
that overran it, littered with sticks
between the boards. I walked across
to the garden, then listened for a bird to turn
the light into a song that would wake
the other birds to their desultory
songs, until a chorus of birds
was singing a dozen different songs
that sounded as one in the overstory.
I stood in a row of corn and heard
a phoebe sing, and then a mocking
bird. But where was yours, my love?
The high, then low, sweet song
to which I sing in return. The one

whose lyrics decry this hour, calling
for darkness instead of song, always
more darkness and a little time.

To a Grieving Daughter

Sing to me about the bees.
Let them buzz around you
like a nimbus as you carry your tune.
They will not sting you if you're not afraid.
I need to hear what I don't expect.
How much you grew to love him
from across the river.
How singing grows from grief.
Give me the news about the bees
swarming from the hive behind
your house the day your father died.
How they clung all day to the pergola
before flying to the hollow of an apple tree.
How you draped their door with a veil,
then grasped the trunk with both your hands
to feel the hum inside your body.
How you hummed your news
throughout the evening that was
their buzz in the dark of the tree.
In the dark of sky as it fell on you.

Pomegranate

I didn't send you the pomegranate to write about,
but to eat.
        It is from *this* world that each seed
counts for a day of life.

Memoir

I willed the knife to hit the mark and it did
sometimes at the point, and stuck. Practice led
to skill until my eyes were covered with a handker-
chief and my beloved straddled a wheel
for all to see as I threw at her to hit
the space between her legs, beside her head,
beneath her arms. This was it, all
or nothing: my life and hers in a mortal art
where every night she was reprieved for having
lived, and I was kissed as she was freed
as part of the act that traveled the country and built
my fame as the man who misses with perfect aim.

Absence

is a face that hangs
in the air, as if the air
were a screen and your heart
the machine that casts the image.

Absence is the shadow
that has broken free of its forms
and wanders the earth.

Absence is a stone, of course.

Absence is the name
the man of faith repeats
in his sleep, and also the woman,
until they too are gone.

Absence is the body the soul creates
from air that masquerades as nothing
throughout the house.

Confessions of a Priest

I said something I can't recall
in the pulpit of the packed cathedral.
How solitary, wrecked, and incorporeal
she rendered me at the altar on which
I prayed like a man and failed. To which
I return alone on Tuesdays with pure
desire to rise like a soul with her
into the ether of the clerestory.
Turn transparent and blue in the glory
of her image in the window that grows newer
with age as the light shines through her.

All the Unlikeness

I detected your scent in the dark
and followed it into the woods
with too much confidence, forgetful
of the beasts who had become estranged
from me and dangerous. I ran
with the stamina of a bear throughout
the night, imagining a song as I ran:
You are my sunshine. My only sunshine.
Your sweetness in the air that was also foul
emboldened me to track you down,
I have exited the parlor of your sheepfold now
with no way back through the open door.

I could wander like this forever until
I disappear, lie down somewhere where
no one can find me in the steppe
then dream my way across the river,
leave only you to tell the story
of my forgiveness and your contumely,
of my transgression and your dark beauty.

What livelihood awaits me now
that I'm obsessed with the memory of you
shaving my back, combing my hair,
kissing my cock? I know I was a fool
for drinking from your spring instead
of the river. I was a man who didn't know
I was a man until I slept with you,
then woke in this dream that I'm still having.
I'm this far down The Road of the Sun
without regard for what anyone thinks
about my love, picking up your scent

that is so strong it has remained in the air
like a flower that continues to bloom.

I sing the song that I made up about your body,
how all of its pieces are less than the whole
I can't describe, how each exquisite part
brings to mind another thing that is nothing
like what I say it is—your breasts twin clouds
that float forever, your lips two figs
I cannot pick, your groin a lamp that burns
in the river—but nonetheless is inside my heart.
I'm this obsessed with all the unlikeness
that you inspire as I wander the hills without
the innocence that was my loneliness.

My Love Is a Leaf

You were standing in the chill October air,
waving to me from your open door.
You were speaking for the leaf that was
your heart-scarlet maple, yellow oak.
You were joining the chorus of leaves
in a voice as clear as the trees were bright.
You were singing the song you'd sung before
ten thousand times from your open door.
I was driving away on Blue Mountain Road
singing to myself, "My love is a leaf
that burns like a tire. My love is a leaf
in the rearview mirror." You were falling
as I sang this made up song. You were
as quiet as a stone on your way back down.

The Double Dream of a Grievous Man

> I slept but my heart was awake.
> —SONG OF SONGS 5:2

I lay beside you again in a bed
that was not our bed but was.
You took me in your arms and said
nothing as the sun shone through
the curtain that was also your dress
drying in the window. I fell asleep
in this dream and dreamed again
of you as you were in your long white dress.
We were making it up in our sleep
between the sheets that were also pages
on which we wrote in invisible ink.
We were happy again for a moment
in the light that shone from the inside
out, but also from above. That filtered
into the room through the dress hanging
in the window as your new garment
so high above it floated as a form
for forms, then turned to light.

Enkidu's Lament

It's the first warm day of spring.
The robins are back and the forsythia is blooming.
The sky is painfully blue.
I'm punished for the slightest emotion.
That "painfully"—I take it back
at the cost of an arm.
But what's an arm when I've got another
for holding you?
Mistakes are measured here in body parts.
This air I breathe is thick with souls
that fill me with what they've lost.
So few bodies remain, lingering at the stile,
forgetting their names.
I would say nothing forever
if silence were forbidden.

Dumuzi's Lament

Where in the valley sleeps my baby?
I hear the chorus of a thousand trees
announce her presence in a distant county.
She has embarked on a dangerous journey
to find her sister beneath the mountains.
"Love is not enough," she cried
like a red-tailed hawk in the cloudless sky.
Enough for what? I wonder.
It was her sister who called her down
to the lowest field where bodies hang on shiny nails.
Where her return depends on my exchange.
I turned to killing when I couldn't find her.
What else was I to do?
The earth is hardly peaceful,
and she has gone to hell.

I Orpheus, I Solomon, I Romeo

I was Orpheus, Solomon, and Romeo
come back from the dead as a fool
who had died for love to walk again
with my beloved, as long, that is,
as I adhered to the terms inscribed
on the soles of my shoes:
"I Orpheus, I Solomon, I Romeo
agree to die again in a different way,
to sleepwalk over a cliff this time
from dreaming awake beside
my gazelle in a little cafe by the sea.
To fall through the sky like a nail
while she converses with me
about nothing that I'll recall,
falling also, or so I think, although
she's flying, sparrow that she is,
until I hit the water and break
my neck. Lie supine on the deep
for a while, beyond critical, then sink
like a bone without even a wave."

Memory Is a Fire

I was shopping for an end to my travails
in the Eschaton Mall when suddenly I spied
my second wife from the Golden Age
in Lord and Taylor. I saw just then
what it was I'd lost, her Eleusinian style,
her beauty from a distance that was also near,
right there but sovereign now in the endless aisle
of millennial blouses. That bedighted.
What was I so sure of as a younger man
to leave her behind? That I would forget
the fire that burned in us like an angel's dress
dipped in oil? That it would burn us clean
like the camps I torched?
What did I know about the coal
inside my heart? How long it burns
like anthracite on the tragic facts.
How nothing's lost inside the dark
at the center of the flames. I needed
to burn for a hundred years to see
what I feel and feel what I see
in the country I won with so much force.

Eros

He rules in exile like a king who hides in public
and writes nothing down.

He replenishes his sources from an underground river
that is the home of the most hardy fishes.

He lives in the mind like a lover in the attic
who won't come down, who needs everything
brought to him in order to survive.

He talks on the phone to the mind
with whom he quarrels and then hangs up
without saying good-bye.

He works out all day on a secret track.
Is vain, vain, vain in short short shorts.

He walks in shackles from which he knows
he can escape at any time, bleeding
from the ankles all over the court.

He dresses in rags but always looks great,
emitting an odor of lilacs and dirt.

He never ages or thinks too much.
Plays the lyre like Orpheus.

He tries to be serious like a child in church
but can't help laughing beneath his breath
at the man in black who won't shut up.

He speaks to the animals like one himself
and sleeps in the trees without falling out.

He has dinner with Death once a week
at the Café Rue where they eat and eat
until Death throws up
and the maitre d' rips up the check.

He searches the Earth in vain
for a love of his own without giving up.

The Double Truth

I still taste you from the time
you painted my tongue
with your scarlet finger.
It cured my heart of innocence,
that single dose, and I have tasted it—
the double truth—ever since:
the bittersweet in the words
I cannot speak but stick
in my mouth like stones
I've learned to talk around.

Curtains

The sheets in your windows
and trees are the linens
we slept in and dreamed.
Now they flap in the breeze
like rags. No rescue
by *The Mercy* enjambs
my heart. No island rhymes
with paradise. My cry
is brief but well rehearsed.
If nothing I say turns
the helm of your oneiric
house, then the wind
that fills your sails with sorrow
is a wind that blows from the north
today and the south tomorrow.

Postdiluvian

I was so busy adding and subtracting
I never did the long division.
Draw for me now the little half house
from across the river to put a number in.
I'll stand at its door that never opens
as the one who becomes the other
no matter how small or large.
Who rises to the roof in the flooding river.

The Mystery

You, but not you as you were
at the start, my other self
I wanted to know, more
than know, also be, joined
as one, now as then,
but different too, still young
but clearer now, almost ready,
so when we gaze at each other
from across the room
we want to say again,
Take me, as if all our days
were one but we had aged
for a reason that lies at the heart
of a secret we cannot tell,
except for some humming
and a little whistling
on the hardest days.

ACKNOWLEDGMENTS

Grateful acknowledgment is made to the following publications, in which these poems first appeared, sometimes in earlier versions: *Agni* ("The Police," "The Thinker"); *Agni Online* ("Trailer"); *American Poetry Review* ("Eros," "Memory Is a Fire"); *Antioch Review* ("Curtains," "What Beauty Knows about Itself"); *Blackbird* ("The Soul Addresses Her Beloved in the Non-Green Zone"); *Christianity and Literature* ("Sunday Calls"); *Cincinnati Review* ("They Are Most at Home"); *Colorado Review* ("Ockham Applies His Razor to the Thought of Aquinas"); *Cortland Review* ("All the Unlikeness," "The Bride as Scout," "The Fire in the Distance"); *Crazyhorse* ("Coyotes," "To a Grieving Daughter," and "A History of Love's Body," under the title "Withdrawal"); *Denver Quarterly* ("Pitch," "The Woe That Is in Friendship"); *5 AM* ("Puritan in Flight"); *Florida Review* ("From the Curriculum of a Serpent"); *Gettysburg Review* ("In a Dark Wood"); *Green Mountains Review* ("The Animals," "April 1," "Storm Cloud"); *Hotel Amerika* ("The Only Road"); *Hudson Review* ("The Silence"); *Hunger Mountain Review* ("At the Socratic Sugarhouse"); *Iowa Review* ("Absence"); *Literary Imagination* ("After Marlowe," "Renunciation"); *Mississippi Review* ("The Double Truth"); *Nightsun* ("Enkidu's Lament"); *P.F.S. Post* ("Club Erebus," "Memoir"); *Poetry East* ("My Love Is a Leaf"); *Prairie Schooner* ("Pomegranate"); *Progressive* ("Dear George"); *Salmagundi* ("Confessions of a Priest"); *Smartish Pace* ("I Orpheus, I Solomon, I Romeo"); *Southern Review* ("After the Storm," "August 17," "The Double Dream of a Grievous Man," "What a Doll Am I"); *TriQuarterly* ("This Ecstasy," "Postdiluvian"); *Willow Springs* ("The Golden Herd," under the title "The Way They Were Lowing"); *Worcester Review* ("First Sex").

I am grateful to the following people for their critical and moral support in the making of this book: Liz deNiord, Bruce Smith, Ed Ochester, Deborah Meade, Ann Walston, Ethan Canin, Stephen Sandy, Thomas Lux, Jacqueline Gens, Marcia Croll, and Ruth Stone.